Earth is Tilting!

by Conrad J. Storad

Science Content Editor:
Kristi Lew

Educational Media

rourkeeducationalmedia.com

Science content editor: Kristi Lew

A former high school teacher with a background in biochemistry and more than 10 years of experience in cytogenetic laboratories, Kristi Lew specializes in taking complex scientific information and making it fun and interesting for scientists and non-scientists alike. She is the author of more than 20 science books for children and teachers.

© 2012 Rourke Educational Media

All rights reserved. No part of this book may be reproduced or utilized in any form or by any means, electronic or mechanical including photocopying, recording, or by any information storage and retrieval system without permission in writing from the publisher.

www.rourkeeducationalmedia.com

To Laurie. Dazzle the world with your kindness!
-- CJS

Photo credits: Cover © Sailorr, Cover logo frog © Eric Pohl, test tube © Sergey Lazarev; Table of Contents © Anton Balazh, Michelangelus; Page 5 © Sailorr; Page 7 © Veniamin Kraskov, Aaron Amat; Page 8 © Veniamin Kraskov, Aaron Amat; Page 9 © Ibooo7, Aaron Amat; Page 11 © somchaij; Page 13 © sebikus; Page 14 © Anton Balazh, Michelangelus; Page 15 © Anton Balazh, Michelangelus; Page 17 © Orla; Page 19 © Ibooo7, sebikus; Page 20 © inginsh; Page 21 © MaszaS

Editor: Kelli Hicks

Cover and page design by Nicola Stratford, bdpublishing.com

Library of Congress Cataloging-in-Publication Data

Storad, Conrad J.
 Earth is tilting! / Conrad J. Storad.
    p. cm. -- (My science library)
 Includes bibliographical references and index.
 ISBN 978-1-61741-750-4 (hard cover) (alk. paper)
 ISBN 978-1-61741-952-2 (Soft cover)
 1. Earth--Rotation--Juvenile literature. 2. Earth--Orbit--Juvenile literature. 3. Seasons--Juvenile literature. I. Title.
 QB633.S759 2012
 525'.35--dc22
                              2011004757

Rourke Educational Media
Printed in the United States of America,
North Mankato, Minnesota

rourkeeducationalmedia.com
customerservice@rourkeeducationalmedia.com • PO Box 643328 Vero Beach, Florida 32964

Table of Contents

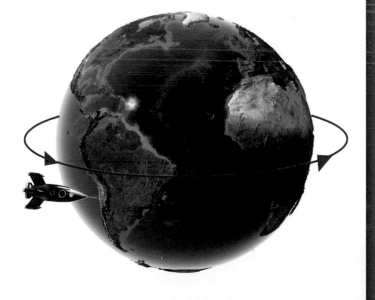

Tilt and Spin

We live on planet **Earth**. It seems like our Earth is holding still, but we know that Earth is a planet moving in space. But, did you know that Earth is **tilted**?

Earth is like a spinning top. It rotates because it formed from a spinning cloud of gas and dust.

5

Earth leans a little to one side. Imagine a straw pushed through the center of an orange. The orange doesn't tilt when the straw is straight up.

Now tilt the straw at an angle. The orange tilts in the same direction. The same thing happens with Earth.

The straw represents Earth's **axis**. The axis is an imaginary line from the North Pole to the South Pole. Earth spins around its tilted axis.

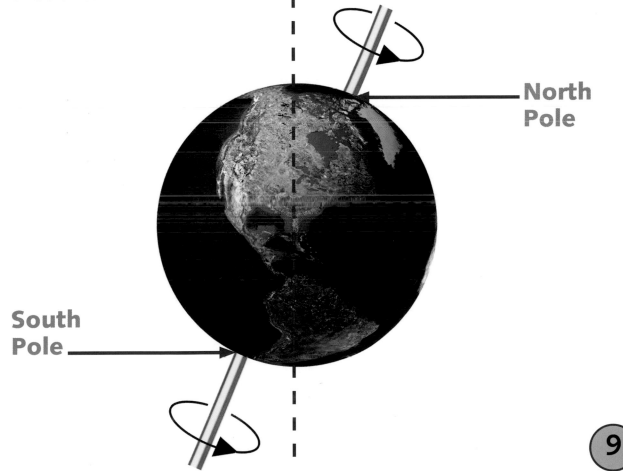

North Pole

South Pole

Day and Night

Earth takes 24 hours to spin one time. We call this period of time one Earth day.

During one day, half of Earth always faces toward the **Sun** and the other half faces away from the Sun.

The spinning motion of Earth is called rotation. It causes the cycle of day and night.

It is daytime on the part of the Earth that faces the Sun. It is nighttime on the part of Earth that faces away from the Sun.

The imaginary line that divides Earth's day side from the night side is called the terminator.

Sun

Earth

terminator

13

Imagine you are on a spaceship looking at Earth. When you look at Earth from the side it spins from left to right.

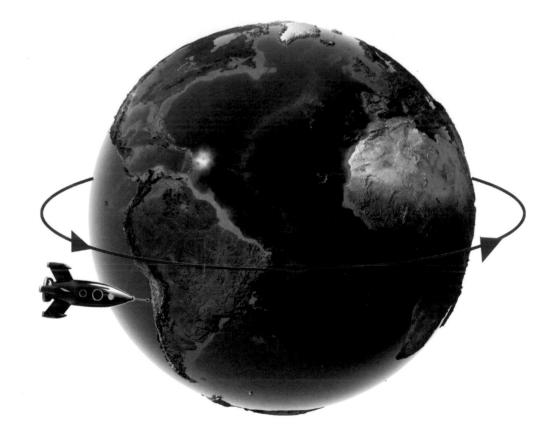

When you look at Earth from the top it spins **counterclockwise**.

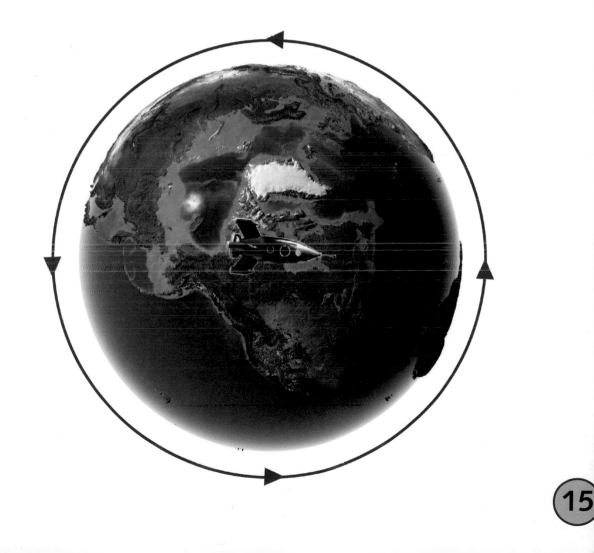

The Reason for Seasons

It takes one year for Earth to complete a single **orbit**. During this time Earth also spins on its axis 365.25 times. One year equals 365 days.

As it orbits the Sun, Earth's tilt causes the seasons. It is summer on the part of the Earth tilted toward the Sun.

It is winter on the part tilted away from the Sun.

The path our Earth travels around the Sun is called its orbit.

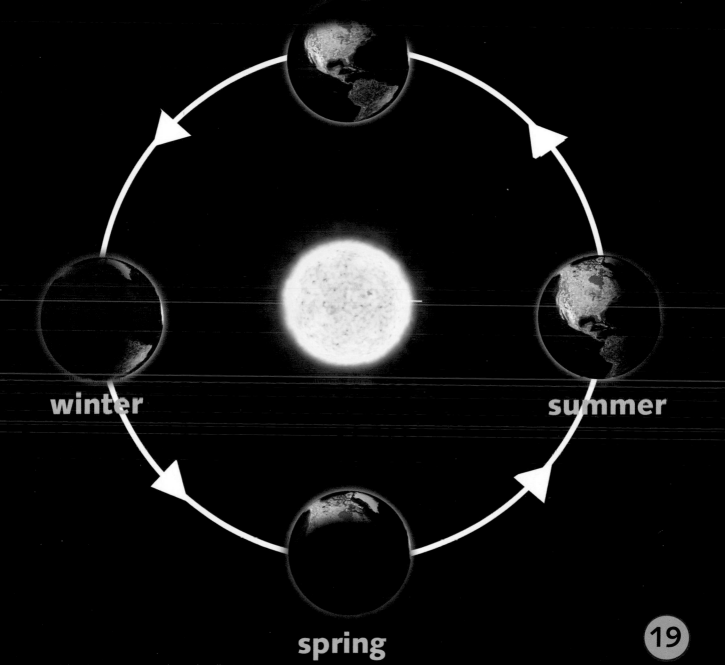

autumn

winter

summer

spring

19

Sun and Earth are not to scale in this illustration

In winter, days get shorter because less direct sunlight reaches the part of Earth tilted away from the Sun.

The temperature gets colder when less direct sunlight shines on the Earth.

In summer, days get longer because more direct sunlight reaches the part of Earth tilted toward the Sun.

Our planet never gets too hot or too cold in one spot because Earth is tilting!

The temperature gets hotter when more direct sunlight shines on the Earth.

SHOW What You Know

1. Name the imaginary line that runs through the center of Earth from top to bottom. Why is it important?

2. How long does it take Earth to spin one time? How long does it take to complete one orbit around the Sun?

3. How does the tilt of Earth cause the seasons?

Glossary

axis (AK-sis): an imaginary line through the middle of an object around which that object spins

counterclockwise (koun-tur-KLAHK-wize): in a direction opposite to the way the hands of a clock move

Earth (URTH): the third planet from the Sun, it is the planet where we live

orbit (OR-bit): the curved path followed by a moon or planet as it circles another planet or the Sun

Sun (SUHN): the star that the Earth and other planets revolve around and that gives us light and warmth

tilted (TILT-ed): leaned, tipped, or slanted to one side

Index

Websites

www.sciencespot.net

www.science.nasa.gov/kids/

www.amazing-space.stsci.edu/

www.spaceplace.nasa.gov/en/kids/

www.fourmilab.ch/earthview/vplanet.html

Photo by Tom Story

About the Author

Conrad J. Storad is the award-winning author of more than 30 books for young readers. He writes about desert animals, plants, creepy crawlers, and planets. Conrad lives in Tempe, Arizona with his wife Laurie and their little double dapple wiener dog, Sophia. They love to explore Arizona's deserts and mountains.